WRECKS AND DISASTERS

Robert Shipley/Fred Addis

Great Lakes Album Series

Vanwell Publishing Limited
St. Catharines, Ontario

Canadian Cataloguing in Publication Data
Shipley, Robert, 1948-
      Wrecks and disasters

(Great Lakes album series)
1st Canadian ed.
Includes bibliographical references.
ISBN 0-920277-77-2

1. Shipwrecks - Great Lakes - History - Pictorial
works. I. Addis, Fred A. (Fred Arthur), 1952-
II. Title. III. Series

   G525.S55 1992   971.3   C92-093541-9

Design Susan Nicholson

Cover: The chaos and terror of a marine disaster is captured in Ernie Taylor's painting of the
Wreck of the Waubano. There were no survivors from the 1879 Georgian Bay tragedy. Taylor had to
speculate about what actually happened. The use of a naive style and elements of impressionistic
detail add a surreal feeling to the scene. The painting was commissioned for a hotel in Collingwood,
Ontario, and now hangs in the Marine Museum of the Great Lakes at Kingston where it is a perennial
favourite with visiting school children. *Marine Museum of the Great Lakes at Kingston.*

CONTENTS

A Deck Awash

The unidentified freighter, on which this picture was taken in the 1940s, probably survived the rough weather it was experiencing. We don't have pictures from the hundreds of Great Lakes vessels that were not so lucky. We can get some idea from this photo, however, of what the conditions that claimed so many boats could be like. The deck that is covered with frothing water would normally have been a couple of metres above the lake surface.

National Archives of Canada C30793

DANGEROUS WATERS

The Great Lakes have long been among the world's busiest waterways. Ship traffic has shared numerous narrow rivers and channels, stood off shores that are often rock and reef strewn and sailed in weather that can be harsh and changeable. As a consequence the waters of the Great Lakes have also been very dangerous.

The era of the famous Spanish treasure galleons pales in comparison to the Great Lakes. In the roughly 170 years between the 1600s and the 1800s when these fabled Spanish ships crossed the Atlantic and Pacific oceans, about forty were lost. In the single shipping season of 1883 on the Great Lakes there were forty shipwrecks.

In one three-day period in November 1905, there were thirty wrecks on Lake Superior alone. And while the cargo of the inland fleets was generally grain, timber, coal and iron ore, rather than gold and silver, people, the most precious cargo of all, were lost in shocking numbers. In 1850 on Lake Erie, well over four hundred people lost their lives.

Water travel on the Great Lakes began thousands of years ago when the first native peoples pushed their sturdy bark craft into the sweet water seas. Europeans adopted the native canoe traditions at first in their search for furs and a way to the Orient. By the late 1600s, however, the building of sailing ships had begun. In these larger vessels the new inland sailors ventured more boldly into the open expanses of the lakes. The results were almost immediate. The very first European vessel on the upper lakes, the *Griffon*, built by the Sieur de LaSalle above Niagara in 1679, disappeared without a trace.

Sailing ships were followed by steam- and diesel-powered vessels on the lakes. Different types of ships were more or less susceptible to various perils. Sailing ships were apt to succumb to gales, fast steamers were more often victims of the unforgiving shoreline, while fire and explosion could claim boats whose machinery was not kept in perfect repair. Collision claimed still others and some simply disappeared without a trace. While the threat of disaster remains ever present, stricter regulations and better design have produced a much improved safety record.

Str. Sharples
May 6 /11

Marine Museum of the Great Lakes at Kingston 982.19.81

John Sharples

The stern of the steamship *John Sharples* shows extensive damage sustained when it ran afoul of Galops Island at the eastern end of Lake Ontario. Parts of the propeller blades have been sheered off. The vessel is seen here in the dry dock at Kingston, Ontario, awaiting repairs in May 1911. It was later towed to Buffalo, New York, rebuilt and survived until the 1940s.

Kidd Collection, Public Archives of Ontario, AO 827

N. P. Clement

The canal-sized chemical tanker *N. P. Clement* was scuttled in Georgian Bay after severe cracks developed in its hull. The ship's seacocks were opened and the *Clement* is shown plunging to the bottom stern first.

C. C. Barnes

Being driven ashore was not always calamitous for the stout and well-built sailing vessels of the nineteenth century. After fetching-up on the beach at Milwaukee in 1894, the *C. C. Barnes* appeared little worse for the wear. A tug is attempting to pull the schooner free.
Manitowoc Maritime Museum

THE LEE SHORE

It is difficult to sink a wooden sailing vessel as long as it has sea room and enough sail to manoeuvre. Schooner barges were schooners with much of their rigging and perhaps even a mast removed. They were loaded with cargo and then towed behind a steam-powered vessel. There were cases where such barges became separated in storms and managed to survive by sailing offshore sometimes for days until rescued.

The real danger for a distressed sailing vessel is not open water or even the weather. The worst danger is the lee shore. In sailing terminology the *lee* is the direction toward which the wind is blowing. The *lee shore* is the coast onto which a sailing vessel will be driven if it is unable to manoeuvre away.

There are of course notable examples of Great Lakes schooners that capsized or foundered in open water. Some of these, such as the *Hamilton* and *Scourge* and the *Alvin C. Clark* are well known because their wrecks were in remarkable states of preservation when found. The *Hamilton* and the *Scourge* foundered in Lake Ontario off what is now St. Catharines, Ontario, during the War of 1812. They rest upright on the bottom with portions of their rigging still intact. When the *Alvin C. Clark* was raised from Green Bay on Lake Michigan, it could almost have been sailed away. Unfortunately it subsequently disintegrated for want of proper conservation.

But such sinkings were generally explainable exceptions. The War of 1812 schooners, though built as merchantmen, had been mounted with extremely heavy cannons and were quite unstable. The *Clark* went down in 1862 during the American Civil War and was undermanned because so many men were absent.

The fact remains that the great majority of sailing vessels wrecked on the Great Lakes came to grief on a lee shore. The relative narrowness of the lakes means that a sailing vessel is virtually always on a lee shore, always just hours or minutes from being driven onto a beach or a rocky ledge should the winds and other conditions conspire against its survival.

Samana

Often the fate of a vessel stranded on a lee shore was sealed even if the crew were lucky enough to escape. A close look at this picture of the little schooner barge *Samana*, ashore near Cleveland, Ohio, in 1892, reveals serious problems. The sagging stern indicates that its back may already be broken.

J. H. Rutter

All too often when a vessel was driven onto a lee shore it meant mortal danger for the hapless crew. Their only hope was to scramble into the rigging, as the crew of the *J. H. Rutter* did when their schooner was wrecked off Grand Haven, Michigan, in 1878. Flying the inverted flag distress signal, they wait for a rescue attempt from shore.

Manitowoc Maritime Museum

Singapore

The angles of the masts show that the *Singapore*, beached near
Kincardine, Ontario, in 1904, is already beginning to break up. The scene
is made more chaotic by the appearance of the deck cargo of lumber
floating loose in the surf around the wreck. One wonders how many
buildings along the shores of the Great Lakes were constructed from
bonanzas of free timber that came ashore following such disasters.
Marine Museum of the Great Lakes at Kingston 984.11.12

Schooners *Baltic* and *Daniel G. Fort*

Sometimes calamity was added to calamity on the lee shore especially during the treacherous gales of November and December. It was 1894 when the Canadian schooner *Baltic*, loaded with 10,000 bushels of barley, failed to make the harbour entrance at Oswego, New York, and was wrecked. Days later the much larger schooner, *Daniel G. Fort*, joined the disintegrating *Baltic* on the same beach. (Oswego was a particularly notorious place for wrecks. See pp. 15 and 61).

Marine Museum of the Great Lakes at Kingston 984.11.152

Margaret Dahl

Manitowoc Maritime Museum

Pictures of wrecks were often taken days after the event when the serenity of the scene belies the violence of the storms that caused them. The horses and wagon on the quiet beach of South Manitou Island, Lake Michigan, are probably off-loading the cargo of the *Margaret Dall* in 1906. The schooner was thirty-nine years old when it was wrecked while engaged in the lumber trade. It had been built in Michigan City, Indiana, for John Caeser of Chicago.

14

Albacore

Prior to being pounded to pieces against the seawall at Oswego, New York, in September 1900, the schooner *Albacore* had served twenty-three seasons on the lakes. The 44-metre (145-foot) vessel was built at Muir Brothers Shipyard in Port Dalhousie, Ontario, in 1872.

Steamer *Collingwood*

Great Lakes Historical Society, Vermilion, Ohio

The *Collingwood* was built in Buffalo in 1852. After running aground in Lake Superior, this illustrated news picture captured the effort to refloat it. Two crewmen can be seen on the forward deck attempting to push the vessel off the rocks with long poles.

RUNNING AGROUND

Steam power added several new dimensions to Great Lakes shipping. A reliable and constant power source, unlike the wind, it allowed vessels to keep regular schedules, make more trips in a given time period and steer direct courses. However, it also meant that if they were off course in the dark or in a fog, they did not go ashore only with the force of the surf and wind as sailing vessels did, but with all the speed generated by their own engines as well. Occasionally this meant that doomed ships drove through the deadly surf and hard up onto a shore where those aboard could reach safety (see pg. 20). More often it resulted in vessels being torn apart on rocks or shoals, making their situations even worse.

There were several reasons why a vessel might stray off course. Even though an increasing number of lighthouses and navigation aids marked the shipping routes on the lakes as the nineteenth century unfolded, ships were still often out of sight of lights. Fog and foul weather increased the chances of losing one's way. Sometimes the ship's compass or the device called a log, used to measure speed, might malfunction. Most often, however, the problem was human error.

Given the uncompromising nature of the ever-near shores of the lakes, and their innumerable islands, the error could be great or slight and the result would be the same. The steamers *Turret Chief* and *L. C. Waldo* were both caught in one of the worst storms in history in November 1913. As the gale grew worse, the captain of the *Turret Chief* thought he was off the north shore of Lake Superior. In fact, he was about 160 kilometres (100 miles) to the south heading straight for the Keweenaw Peninsula. At almost the same time the master of the *Waldo*, in spite of having the wheelhouse of his vessel torn off by a giant wave and having to steer using a hand compass, was only a few hundred metres (a half mile) off course. Both steamers, nevertheless, ran aground.

Regional Collection, The University of Western Ontario

Algoma

The Canadian Pacific Railway steamship, *Algoma*, was one of three built in Scotland and sailed to Canada. They were cut in half at Montreal, towed through the canals to Buffalo and rejoined. In only its second season running between Owen Sound and Port Arthur, Ontario, in 1885, the *Algoma* ran aground at Isle Royale during a fierce November storm. What had taken labourers weeks to do, namely separate the ship into two parts, Lake Superior did in minutes. Thirty-seven people went to their deaths in the icy waters. Thirteen were inspired to hold on through the night by Captain Moore and survived to be rescued.

Hattie B. Pereue

Trying to outrun a Lake Michigan storm in October 1902, the steamer *Hattie Pereue* struck a sandbar off the harbour entrance at Holland, Michigan. All the crewmen were rescued, but the vessel was a total loss.

Lafayette

During the last three days of November 1905, Lake Superior experienced the worst storm in its recorded history. Particularly hard hit was the Pittsburgh Steamship Line. Ore carriers towing fully loaded barges often meant doubled losses. When the *Lafayette* crashed into the rocks near Two Harbors, Minnesota, her barge *Manila* followed. Their crews, miraculously, were able to scramble to safety ashore. The impact broke the *Lafayette* in two.

Manitowoc Maritime Museum

Crescent City

Not far from the place where the *Lafayette* came ashore, the steamer *Crescent City* was also grounded. Here again, the crew managed to get ashore using ladders. The temperature of the water can be imagined when one realizes that there are icicles hanging from the hull. This vessel was to survive the 1905 storm only to experience further troubles later (see pg. 53).

Mataafa

Great Lakes Historical Society, Vermilion, Ohio

The most spectacular victim of the 1905 storm was the big ore carrier *Mataafa*. As the storm began to build, the *Mataafa* left Duluth with her barge, *Nasmyth*, in tow. After some hours on the lake, Captain Humble decided to turn back. He knew he could never get his tow safely past the breakwalls of the harbour in the mountainous seas so he cut it loose. Then, just as *Mataafa* was almost through the breakwalls, it was caught by the waves and smashed first against one wall and then the other. The big boat was pushed back out into the lake by the surge and cast up on the rocks where the whole city of Duluth could see its agony. Nine men froze to death aboard the stern section of the ill-fated vessel. The *Nasmyth* managed to get its anchors to hold and rode out the storm.

Monarch

In December 1906, the passenger and freight steamer *Monarch* struck Blake Point, Isle Royale, Lake Superior, in a blinding snowstorm. Soon only nine metres (30 feet) of the bow remained above water. Passengers went hand-over-hand on a line tied to a tree ashore. Of the sixty people aboard, only sixteen men and three women were rescued thirty-six hours later.

Alexandria

Public Archives of Ontario ACC 6744 S11528

The paddle wheeler *Alexandria* was en route from Picton, Ontario, to Toronto in 1915 when it ran into difficulties off the Scarborough Bluffs. The cruel pounding of Lake Ontario soon took its toll on the wreck, creating a sort of cross sectional view of the steamer's machinery as it tore away the paddle boxes and most of the cabin. The vessel was insured for $75,000.

Pilgrim

Institute for Great Lakes Research, Bowling Green State University US 150433

When strong spring ice opened the seams in the hull of the *Pilgrim* in April 1907, the combination passenger and package freight steamer was beached at Fort Gratoit, Michigan. All thirty-four persons aboard were rescued.

Huronic

Not all cases of ships running aground occurred in the gales of autumn. The *Huronic* was one of the Canada Steamship Lines passenger steamers that worked on the Upper Lakes in this century. It was built in 1901 at Collingwood, Ontario. In this striking picture the *Huronic* is seen high and dry on the rocks of Lucille Island in Lake Superior in August 1928. It was successfully refloated.

Manitowoc Maritime Museum

George M. Cox

It was the spring of 1933 when the *George M. Cox* fetched up on Rock of Ages Reef off the western end of Isle Royale in Lake Superior. The *Cox* was built in 1901 at Toledo, Ohio, as the *Puritan*. All 118 people got ashore and spent an uncomfortable but safe night at the lighthouse before being rescued. The vessel was not as lucky. Shortly after this picture was taken, the *Cox* slid off the reef and sank.
Regional Collection, The University of Western Ontario

Erie

Buffalo and Erie County Historical Society

The handsome paddle wheeler *Erie* set out from Buffalo on an August evening in 1841 bound for Cleveland, Detroit and Chicago. Aboard were over two hundred people, many of them Swiss and German immigrants carrying all their possessions and a good deal of cash in silver and gold coins. No one knows how it happened, but within minutes the whole ship was engulfed in flames. Only twenty-nine people survived, including the captain, one woman and the cook who left us the most complete eye witness account of the tragedy.

FIRES & EXPLOSIONS

An ever-present danger in the confined spaces of any vessel designed and built for water transportation is fire. Fire could be equally devastating whether a vessel was underway in open water as was the *Erie* in 1841 (see page opposite), or when a ship was alongside the supposed safety of a quay, as in the case of the *Noronic* in 1949 (see pp. 34 and 35).

When both ocean and lake ships were built entirely of wood they could be totally consumed by flames once a fire began. Even when the construction of ships' hulls changed to iron and then steel, the interiors of passenger ships consisted largely of decorative wooden panels and furnishings. Since these were almost always painted or varnished they provided not only ample fuel for fires but produced deadly smoke and toxic fumes. Once fire had taken hold of a ship, however, even the metal itself burned or became so hot that no one could survive in its presence.

Fires could begin in the holds where various cargoes were carried, in the galley where cooking was done, in the engine room or anywhere by the carelessness of some passenger or crewmen. Following disasters in the nineteenth century, investigations were seldom able to establish the precise origins of fires since the vessels were often complete losses. By the time of such conflagrations as the *Northumberland* burning at Port Dalhousie, Ontario, in 1949 and the *Noronic* the same year, officials were able to determine causes and enact regulations that helped prevent future occurrences.

The advent of steam boilers in ships producing high-pressure steam carried through a maze of pipes posed an entirely new danger— explosion. Early in the era of steam, when the technology had not been perfected, exploding boilers were a particular problem. Even later when steam was commonplace, any lapse in maintenance or attempt to push a boiler's use beyond its age could lead to disaster. Exploding steam boilers are suspected as a cause in some of the mysterious disappearances of vessels such as the *Bannockburn* which went missing on Lake Superior in 1902 (see pg. 45).

Arizona

The existence of chemicals in dangerous concentrations was relatively new in 1887 when the steamer *Arizona* set off from Marquette, Michigan, on its last trip of the season. In the rough seas some containers of acid broke loose and started a fire below decks. Deadly fumes made fighting the fire impossible as the vessel headed back to port. The captain rammed the burning ship into the breakwall and allowed the crew to jump off. The *Arizona*, still under a full head of steam, pushed along the breakwall as if in pursuit of the escaping crew before running up on the shore and burning to the waterline.

Dover and Erie

In February 1929 a latter-day namesake of the ill-fated *Erie* was laid up for the winter at Ecorse, Michigan, along with the paddle wheeler *Dover*. When flames swept the two vessels the *Erie* became a total loss. The *Dover*, which had enjoyed previous careers under the names *Frank E. Kirby* and *Silver Spray*, subsequently was repaired. A victim of hard economic times, it lay idle until 1932 when fire again destroyed the fine old vessel. It had been built in 1890 and named for Kirby, the famous designer of many of the most beautiful paddle-wheel steamers on the Great Lakes.

Hamonic

The *Hamonic* was one of the well-appointed but ill-fated passenger ships of the Canada Steamship Lines fleet (see *Huronic*, pg. 26 and *Noronic*, pp. 34 and 35). It was early on a July morning 1945 when *Hamonic* came alongside the docks at Sarnia, Ontario. It was on its weekly trip from Detroit to the Upper Lakes with a complement of happy holidayers aboard. Unfortunately a fire that began in a coal pile on the dock soon spread and doomed the ship. In this picture the extent of the fire near the Blue Water Bridge can be seen from a distance.

Regional Collection, The University of Western Ontario

Hamonic

Regional Collection, The University of Western Ontario

The quick action of Captain Horace L. Beaton, along with the heroics of several other people, averted a certain disaster. The captain ordered the ship into reverse and so pulled it away from the burning dock. Some of the passengers were rescued by a steam shovel operator who repeatedly lowered the bucket of his machine onto the deck and lifted groups of them to safety. Not a single life was lost but the vessel was a complete write-off.

Noronic

During the early hours of 17 September 1949, 139 people lost their lives when the passenger ship *Noronic* was gutted by fire at the dockside in Toronto, Ontario. The fire began in a linen closet.

Institute for Great Lakes Research, Bowling Green State University C 134 014

Institute for Great Lakes Research, Bowling Green State University C134014

Noronic

It seemed inconceivable that such a horrendous loss of life could have occurred right beside the dock, but most of the passengers were asleep when the fire broke out. Regulations enacted following the disaster spelled the end for passenger ships with highly flammable wooden superstructures. The burned-out hulk of the once stately *Noronic* was towed to Hamilton, Ontario, and scrapped.

E. M. Peck

Faulty boilers were blamed for the spectacular explosion of the steam barge *E. M. Peck* at Racine, Wisconsin, in June 1913. Four of the vessel's crew of eighteen were killed in the blast that rocked the entire downtown section of the port.

E. M. Peck

The force of the explosion blew one of the vessel's massive Scottish boilers completely out of the hull and into a nearby coal yard. Surprisingly the ship was rebuilt and remained in service under the name *Malton* until it was scrapped in 1935 (see inset).

Institute for Great Lakes Research, Bowling Green State University US 135983

Lady Elgin

The lookout on the timber schooner *Augusta* had spotted the lights of the *Lady Elgin* about twenty minutes before the two vessels collided on a windy but clear night in September 1860. The paddle-wheel steamer was headed from Chicago to Milwaukee carrying a large party of political revellers caught up in pre-Civil War election campaigning. The *Lady Elgin* went to pieces and 297 people drowned. Days later the engines and boilers broke loose from the sunken vessel, allowing the ghostly hull to float to the surface.

COLLISIONS & MYSTERIOUS DISAPPEARANCES

It would seem that collisions between ships in the busy waters of the Great Lakes would most frequently have occurred in narrow confines such as the Pelee Passage at the western end of Lake Erie. In fact, that did happen with the steamer *Morning Star* and the schooner *Courtlandt* in 1868 and again in 1944 with the *Phillip Minch* and *Frank E. Vigor*, just to name two incidents in that location.

But collisions also occurred with an ominous frequency in the open waters of the lakes. The most common explanation for this is simply human error. Contemporary accounts of the August night in 1852, when the fifth worst disaster in Great Lakes history took place, indicate that the weather was calm and, in spite of slight haze, the stars were visible. There is little reason why two large, brightly lit steamers could not have seen one another. But the brand-new propeller *Ogdensburg*, nevertheless, smashed into the palatial paddle wheeler *Atlantic* sending it to the bottom with a loss of nearly 250 lives.

While vessels colliding and sinking is an obvious enough disaster, there are many ships that have simply vanished from the surface of the lakes with no explanation at all. Few things are as perplexing to observers of the lakes or as difficult for the loved ones of those lost in these mysterious disappearances.

Harry Stewart was the only survivor of the wreck of the *Western Reserve* in 1892. He reported that the deck of the doomed vessel cracked amidships. Enough accounts such as Stewart's survive to lead many to suspect hull failure as the culprit in numerous mysterious disappearances of Great Lakes boats.

Ocean

The evidence of collision is clear in the bow of the propeller *Ocean*. The vessel survived this incident only to burn to the waterline at Port Dalhousie, Ontario, in 1904.

Public Archives of Ontario ACC 4122 52203

Fontana

The schooner barge F*ontana*, while in tow of the steamer *Kaliyuga*, collided with the barge *Santiago* off Point Edward, Ontario, when entering the St. Clair River in August 1900. Five crewmen perished when the vessel went down. The stern remained above the water and posed a hazard to navigation. The sunken hull was dynamited to clear the channel.

Alpena

The *Alpena* is one of those mystery ships that simply disappeared without a trace on Lake Michigan one October day in 1880. Somewhere between sixty and one hundred people perished. Careful records of how many passengers were aboard a vessel were not kept in those days. The painting is based partly on conjecture and partly on an account given by Captain Olson of the schooner *Holmes* who saw the steamer in distress before it vanished. It is recorded as the eleventh worst loss of life in lakes history.

City of Cleveland III

The *City of Cleveland III* was one of the fleet of huge passenger-carrying paddle wheelers built in the early part of the twentieth century for the luxury trade on the Great Lakes. It had seven decks and could carry 3,500 passengers. It was one of the last of its breed still in service in 1950 when it was rammed by the Norwegian freighter *Ravnefjell* while crossing Lake Huron. Five passengers were killed and a dozen others were injured while most passengers slept. The damage was not irreparable, but the *City of Cleveland III* was towed to Buffalo and never saw service again before being scrapped in 1955.

Great Lakes Historical Society, Vermilion, Ohio

Marquette & Bessemer No. 2

In the days when rail transport was all important, there were complex interconnecting systems that made cross-lake car ferries economical. One of these links ran across Lake Erie between Conneaut, Ohio, and Port Stanley, Ontario. Loaded with rail cars, the big ferry *Marquette & Bessemer No. 2* disappeared without prior hint of difficulty or warning on 9 December 1909. The entire crew of thirty-six was lost. The vessel pictured here was the replacement for the ill-fated ferry. It was of the same dimensions and was given the same name.

Mr. Christopher Andreae

Bannockburn

The Scottish-built, steel freighter *Bannockburn* disappeared on Lake Superior in November 1902. Legend has it that many sailors transiting those same frigid waters have seen visions of the *Bannockburn*, its three masts and tall stack pitching in the waves. Only two pieces of wreckage from the vessel were ever found. All that remains is a plaque on the Anglican church wall in Port Dalhousie, Ontario, the home port for some of the crew.

St. Catharines Historical Museum L 2126

Charles S. Price

Sixteen vessels and 244 lives were lost between the 8th and 11th of November 1913 during the worst storm on Lake Huron within recorded history. No one will ever know where on the lake or when during those desperate days all of the ships vanished. The hull of the bulk carrier *Charles S. Price* was found floating upside down near the southern end of the lake when the winds finally abated. Engineer Milton Smith was called to identify the bodies that came ashore. He had left the *Price's* crew days before on the premonition of impending disaster.

Edmund Fitzgerald

In 1975, just when the many years of disaster and shipwrecks on the Great Lakes seemed to be passing into distant memory, a new chapter in the story was added. Probably none of the older tales are as well known to people today as the mysterious sinking of the giant iron ore carrier *Edmund Fitzgerald*. The *Fitzgerald* went down near Lake Superior's Whitefish Bay with the loss of all twenty-nine mariners aboard. But the story is not a new or unique one, just one of the latest in a long, long tradition.

St. Magnus

Great Lakes Historical Society, Vermilion, Ohio

The wooden propeller *St. Magnus* capsized at its mooring in Cleveland harbour. It was later righted and returned to service.

CANAL AND DOCKSIDE MISHAPS

One might think that the calm confines of a harbour or the controlled setting of a ship canal was the safest of places for vessels, mariners and passengers alike. Nothing could be further from the truth on certain tragic occasions. Some of the worst disasters that the lakes have known took place a mere step away from dry land.

The canals, especially the Welland that bypassed Niagara Falls after 1829 and the Soo which opened between Lakes Huron and Superior in 1855, were incredibly busy waterways. Wherever else vessels visited on the Great Lakes, they almost all passed through one of these bottlenecks. Considering the sheer number of transits, the safety record was probably good, but when accidents did occur they could be quite spectacular.

Perhaps it was the very notion that the dockside was inherently safe that led to some of the lapses of judgment which created catastrophies of the scale of the *Eastland* when it capsized in Chicago in 1915 (see pg. 52). Generally only a skeleton crew is left aboard a vessel while it is docked, limiting emergency responses.

As with most other aspects of Great Lakes shipping life, a better understanding of the causes of accidents and stricter regulations have greatly reduced the incidents and severity of canal and dockside mishaps. The other reason for reduced problems, and this is perhaps a sadder note, is the fact that there are just many fewer ships in the lakes than there used to be.

Winnie Wing

Not all the action connected with marine mishaps was on the water. This picture of the schooner *Winnie Wing,* lying submerged in the Napanee River in eastern Ontario, was part of the legal evidence in a court case.

Manitowoc Maritime Museum

Ann Arbor No. 4

The railroad car ferry *Ann Arbor No. 4* had a long string of mishaps after being built in Cleveland, Ohio, in 1906. It ran aground several times in various places, but suffered one of its worst insults in 1909 when taking on gondola cars loaded with iron ore at Manistique, Michigan. Too many cars were put on one side and the ferry capsized. It was righted and later renamed the *City of Cheboygan*.

Manitowoc Maritime Museum

Eastland

The tragedy of the *Eastland* stands to this day as the greatest disaster in Great Lakes history. It was early on a Saturday morning in July 1915 when the popular steamer rolled over and sank in the Chicago River just as it was leaving for a day excursion. Although it had been said for years that the vessel was unsafe, nothing before had ever happened to confirm the rumours. In the end it was determined that an engineer had improperly filled the water ballast tanks and that, along with the considerable overcrowding, had led to its instability. Of the 2,500 people on board, 835 lost their lives. The courts judged that the *Eastland's* owners, St. Joseph-Chicago Steamship Company, were not legally liable for the deaths.

52

Great Lakes Historical Society, Vermilion, Ohio

Crescent City

Because the lock gates of a canal hold back hundreds of tons of water, the danger of disaster is always present. Considering the thousands of uneventful canal transits, however, the safety record is almost perfect. On 9 June 1909 the bulk carrier *Crescent City* rode a wave of water through the Soo locks when the lower lock gates burst after being struck by an up-bound freighter. The passenger ship *Assiniboia* preceded the *Crescent City* through the breached lock and into the lower St. Mary's River. Fully loaded at the time, the *Crescent City* escaped with little damage (see also pg. 21).

Tragedy at Lock 22

A more tragic lock gate incident occurred on the Welland Canal near St. Catharines in June 1912. Three boys who were fishing below Lock 22 were drowned when the steamer *La Canadienne* failed to stop on its entry into the lock chamber and smashed through the gates releasing a fatal wave of water on the unsuspecting anglers.

St. Catharines Historical Museum N 2208

Steelton and the Port Robinson Bridge

In the early morning hours of 25 August 1974, the ore carrier *Steelton* struck the east tower of Bridge 12 at Port Robinson on the Welland Canal. The bridge span toppled into the canal, blocking traffic for weeks. The *Steelton* was towed back to Port Colborne at the southern end of the canal for repairs to its damaged bow and wheelhouse. The bridge was never replaced and the two parts of the small community remain separated.

rescuing the
Pacific Dec. 1861
J.G. Howard

Schooner *Pacific*

Public Archives of Ontario ACC 2304 S4296

The kind of gallant rescue that makes for stirring stories was acted out when the schooner *Pacific* was wrecked off the west end of Toronto in December 1861. A well-known local oarsman named Thomas Tinning is credited with saving the crew by getting a lifeline to them. The picture that commemorated the event was painted by a prominent Torontonian named John G. Howard. His famous house, Colborne Lodge in High Park, still overlooks the scene where the rescue occurred.

RESCUES

Wherever danger, accidents and disasters occur, human courage and stamina rise to match them. The story of shipwrecks and disasters on the Great Lakes is replete with tales of survival and rescue that balance with inspiration the despair that otherwise accompanies these tragedies.

A quintessential story of heroism and rescue was acted out at Long Point on the north shore of Lake Erie. Dozens of vessels have come to grief on this sandy peninsula that stretches almost halfway across the lake. During a blinding snowstorm in 1854 the schooner *Conductor* was driven ashore. The Becker family were the only settlers in the area and Abigail Becker was home alone with her children. She built a fire on the beach as a sign of hope to the sailors clinging to rigging of their disintegrating vessel. She encouraged them to swim ashore. One after another they tried, only to sink with exhaustion in the surf, and one after another she waded in and pulled them to safety.

For her heroism "Mother Becker" was given awards and gifts of money. She is remembered in poems, historic plaques and has a local hospital wing named in her honour. She is only one of countless people, however, who have braved the dangers of the lakes to save others.

To the lifesaving services on both the Canadian and American sides of the lakes go much of the praise for daring rescues. Some of these men, especially those in the U.S. Coast Guard, were professionals. Many more, such as the boat crew at Port Stanley, Ontario, who rescued the sailors of the stricken schooner *Mineral State* in November 1902, were volunteers.

Pelee Island Lifeboat Crew

Thousands of men, mostly volunteers like these members of the Pelee Island lifesaving station, stood ready over the years to risk their lives in the effort to save others. In the days before compact reliable boat engines, it was only the muscles of hearty mariners that could take a lifeboat where it was needed. Harbour tugs might be called upon to tow the lifeboats to a ship in distress, but the death-defying dash to the side of a sinking ship to pluck the crew to safety was the domain of the lifeboat crew. Boats like this one were supposedly self-righting, should they be capsized, and self-bailing as can be seen by the row of openings along the side.

National Archives of Canada PA 119817

Rocket

The crew of this Buffalo lifeboat seem to have arrived a bit late to rescue anyone from the sunken propeller *Rocket*, but it is undoubtedly a picture from some time after the event. We can see the horse-drawn rig that was used to bring the boat to where it was needed. Many such lifeboats were stationed around the lakes.

Christy Ann Morrison

It is difficult to put a human face on disasters that happened long ago. But because of her notoriety we have this picture of Christy Ann Morrison, the only female survivor of the ill-fated steamer *Asia*. The vessel went down in Georgian Bay while en route to Manitoulin Island in 1882. After being rescued by a local Indian, Miss Morrison went on the speaking circuit where she sold copies of this evocative portrait.

Dixon, National Archives of Canada PA 120552

Tug *E. J. Redford* and Schooner *Flora Emma*

All rescues have noble intent but not all were successful. When the schooner *Flora Emma* broke away from the box factory dock in Oswego, New York, during a visit to that port in the 1890s, the crew were in the town buying oysters. Only the mate's wife and a young boy were aboard. The tug *Eliza J. Redford* attempted a rescue but lost power and was wrecked itself. Captain Redford of the tug lost his own life, but the schooner's passengers were saved.

Marine Museum of the Great Lakes at Kingston 984.11.145

Argo

We can appreciate the fear in the face of the young passenger in the breaches buoy. The child is being brought ashore from the stranded steamer *Argo* off Ottawa Beach, Michigan, in 1913. A member of the lifesaving crew on shore had braved the icy waters to get to the ship to rig the breaches buoy. All the passengers and crew were saved.

FURTHER READING

Bowen, D. T. *Memories of the Lakes*. Cleveland, OH: Freshwater Press Inc., 1969.

Boyer, D. *Great Stories of the Great Lakes*. New York: Dodd, Mead & Co., 1966.

Greenwood, J. O. *Namesakes 1900-1909* (Also *Namesakes 1910-1919, Namesakes 1920-1929, Namesakes 1930-1935*). Cleveland, OH: Freshwater Press Inc., 1986.

Kemp, P. *The Oxford Companion to Ships and the Sea*. London: Oxford University Press, 1976.

Kuttruff, K. *Ships of the Great Lakes: A Pictorial History*. Detroit: Wayne State University Press, 1976.

Metcalfe, W. *Canvas & Steam On Quinte Waters*. Picton, ON: Prince Edward County Historical Society, 1968.

———. *Marine Memories*. Picton, ON: Gazette Publishing Co. (1971) Ltd., 1975.

Ratigan, W. *Great Lakes Shipwrecks & Survivals*. Grand Rapids, MI: Wm. B. Eerdmans Publishing Co., 1983.

Van der Linden, P., ed. *Great Lakes Ships We Remember* (Also *Great Lakes Ships We Remember II*). Cleveland, OH: Freshwater Press Inc., 1979.

ACKNOWLEDGEMENTS

The authors would like to give special thanks, as always, to their wives and families for their continuing support in all their projects. Vanwell Publishing is to be thanked for their work. Without the efforts of the volunteers and staffs of the following archives and collections, books such as this would simply not be possible: Buffalo and Erie County Historical Society; Bowling Green State University, Institute for Great Lakes Research; Manitowoc Maritime Museum; The Great Lakes Historical Society, Vermilion, Ohio; St. Catharines Historical Museum; National Archives of Canada; Public Archives of Ontario; Marine Museum of the Great Lakes at Kingston; Marine Museum of Upper Canada, Toronto; Southwestern Ontario Regional Collection, The University of Western Ontario in London. Our thanks as well are due to Mr. Christopher Andreae of London, Ontario, Mr. Skip Gillham of Vineland, Ontario, and Mr. Cec Mitchell of the Welland *Evening Tribune* for the use of their picture collections.

INDEX